Watching Her G

The Beauty and Tragedy of Alzheimer's Disease Captured in a Daughter's Poetry

Printed in the United States of America

ISBN - 978-0-692-89242-8

This book is in honor and memory of my mom
whose life was so much more than poetry.

She left fingerprints of grace and bravery on our lives.

~

And to my cousin, Nancy - when I asked you for help, you
didn't even hesitate. Your creative images so powerfully
transcribe emotions into photos. Family is what it's all about.

Other Dedications

To my dad for showing what marriage is really all about with your everlasting love and tireless devotion.

To Bill, my husband, for nudging me to write this book, for your endless support of me and my family and for being my always and forever. There aren't enough words for you.

To Darryl, our son, your care and concern for not only your grandma, but the whole family were just what I needed some days. You are my sunshine.

To everyone who listened to me at all hours as well as those who encouraged me and supported and prayed for our family. I can't thank you enough.

Table of Contents

(Continued)

"It occurred to me that at one point it was like I had two diseases.
- one was Alzheimer's,
and the other was knowing I had Alzheimer's."
Terry Pratchett

"Today is the best day I could ever have."
Anonymous

It's important to me that I explain how this book came to be.

One late evening I was sitting in my home office talking with my dad about my mom's daily events, just as we did almost every night. Throughout the progression of my mom's disease, I felt that I had to separate the emotional daughter from the logical, decision-making side of myself. If I was going to be the best advocate for my mom, then my feelings couldn't get in the way.

I hung up the phone and the next thing I knew there was a poem on my computer. I read what I had written and was pretty shocked because I don't like to read poetry and even though I do like to write short pieces, writing poetry was never on my radar. I have come to believe that the poems are God given and God driven. To this day, I don't set out to write a poem. I am merely the person who puts them on the page.

The poetry was meant to be a private diary kept to record my feelings about slowly losing my mom. They also turned out to be helpful to others in their journeys with their loved ones. A few of the poems were written as requests from others and are not directly related to my mom.

I have read my poetry at various support groups, to family members, to medical staff and to all kinds of caregivers. If you are close to someone with Alzheimer's Disease, you too, will recognize the dark humor, reflection and gut-wrenching and raw experiences.

My utmost respect goes to those in the trenches of caring for and loving someone with this disease. Alzheimer's disease has no cure, it doesn't get easier with time and you'll probably wish current behaviors you want to go away would come back once they're gone. My greatest fear was that she would be afraid and feel alone. There was such a deep, deep sorrow that this was happening to her and we, her family, could not make it different.

Learn everything you can about how this disease works on the brain. Enjoy the little moments and love with all your might. I found that by being intimately involved in a caretaker role and having no expectations about how each interaction would go, I was able to love her where she was, even through the toughest days. I knew that she was not responsible for difficult times and that often my loving her turned things around. We had many special days and nights together and she loved me to the end, just as my love for her grew in ways I couldn't have imagined. Each day was the best day ever, for who knew what tomorrow would bring.

Ann Childress

"Caregiving often calls us to lean into love we didn't know was possible. "
Tia Walker, author

When someone you love calls and wants to read you the first poem they have ever written, you listen. When that poem pours out a sea of raw emotion in a poignant and relative way to their mother's journey with Alzheimer's disease, you really listen. And finally, when they ask you to partner with them in a book, adding your photography to their poetry pages, you say "Of course, Ann."

I didn't know my Aunt Laura as well as I knew her daughter, Ann Marie. As a child, I gave brief hugs to aunts and then hung out with the cousins my age. Candidly, I was lovingly fascinated with Ann. She was smart and funny, precise and silly, structured and cantankerous all rolled into one. She looked so innocent but was really much deeper and more outspoken than any other kid I knew. As an introvert, I loved that about her. And I used to think that because she was one year older, she obviously must know way more than me due to her age.

When Aunt Laura's wrestling match with Alzheimer's disease became more evident, Ann's poetry started coming to her and she shared it with me. We chatted about her dueling experience as being a loving daughter to her mother at the same time she was carrying out a different daughter role for her father in helping him make difficult decisions about his wife. The poetry kept coming, never forced, never planned, just written as it arrived with each new experience. And as she continued to read her poetry, that childhood fascination with Ann came back. This was amazing stuff and we both knew God was smack dab in the center of it.

Ann's poetic observation and creatively worded response to her mother's deterioration reminds me of how important it is for us to process our lives as they are happening.

Watching a parent decline, whether it be 'old age' or something much harsher like Alzheimer's disease, brings on an adult role that tries to distract us from what we must also experience emotionally. Ann's gift of poetry was therapeutic for her, for me in remembering my parents and what I know with all my heart to be true – for others who will soon read this book.

Nancy Merkling

'SHE' Rolls in Like the Tide

There was a slow transition from mom to 'SHE'.
No particular day when 'SHE' arrived.
'SHE' snuck up on us like the tide moving on the beach.
First it met our feet and we giggled a bit
As frigid water washed over them.
The tide won and our chilled toes sank into the sand.

Sentences started missing words.
Things were forgotten.
Our ankles were next.
It was no use as we tried to outrun the foamy water.
The incoming tide with its unpredictable rogue wave
Caught us off guard.

We talked as if 'SHE' wasn't in the room.
How is 'SHE' today?
When did 'SHE' get up?
The tide surged up to our knees.
There was no escaping it.

Wave after wave until we were totally consumed
By the incessant sea.
Wholly engulfed by the relentless breakers.
Did 'SHE' remember you today?
Did 'SHE' eat?

The interminable waves washed over us like clockwork.
They saturated us until we were chilled to the bone.
The brilliant sun shone like a farce. Mocking us.

Our memories sank with each wave.
Hope swept out with the tide.
No escaping it.
The sea had won.

Who is She?

Daughter

      Sister

            Friend

              Wife

                Mother

                    Aunt

                       Grandmother

                              L

                              o

                              s

                              t

Frustration

Today I'm going to count exactly how many times
She asks the same questions.
To count how many times I repeat the same thing.
Just. Like. She's. Two.
But she's not and it's not cute.
They say to answer the 10th time just like the first.
No tone. No teenage eye rolling.
Did you ever try that?

Today I'll try not to notice that she's sitting on a towel.
Or become repulsed over the wet spot on her pants.
Or that I'm now sitting in the chair she was in.

Today when I take her out to lunch and I ask her
What she wants to eat,
I'll remember to read only two things on the menu
That I know she likes.
I won't confuse her with too many suggestions.

Today when I walk into her room,
I'll remember to tell her who I am.
Not just my name, but that I am her daughter.
I'll also remind myself that if she thinks of me as someone else,
Well, that'll be OK, too.

Today I'll remember that she has a brain disease.
That she's not being funny or stupid.
She's not doing any of this intentionally.
She is still my mom who loves me.
She's lost her filtering capacity.
She doesn't want to be this way.

Sometimes she's embarrassed.
Sometimes she's depressed.
Sometimes she's loud and obnoxious.
Sometimes she may hit or kick you,
Or even throw you out of the room.

Frustration.
It's not only yours.
It's hers, too.

Hand Ballet

It's night and shadows loom large
As I sit by your bed watching how you sleep.
I used to recognize you, but no more.
I'm once again getting to know the new you.

You're peaceful now unlike hours ago
When the dragons wouldn't be slayed,
And no amount of monster spray would send them away.

As you go deeper into sleep the most beautiful ballet begins.
Your frail, bruised hands that made a house a home,
Are performing an intricate dance in the air.
I watch, entranced by the exquisiteness of the choreography.

I look at your face to be sure that you're not spoofing me.
What I see is beauty in your brokenness.
Innocence of a child.
Such peacefulness that I wish you'd never awaken.
For the dragons and monsters aren't only under your bed,
They rarely leave your fading days.

Yet, here in the dark, while you sleep,
Where the shadows loom large,
There's such beauty watching the most intricate hand ballet.
More splendid than that of principal dancers
Engaged in a pas de deux.

Hands that move together then separate.
Hands that circle the air with the effortless dance
Of a man and woman in love,
Or the love of a mother for her child.
Here in the dark, there's beauty beyond compare.

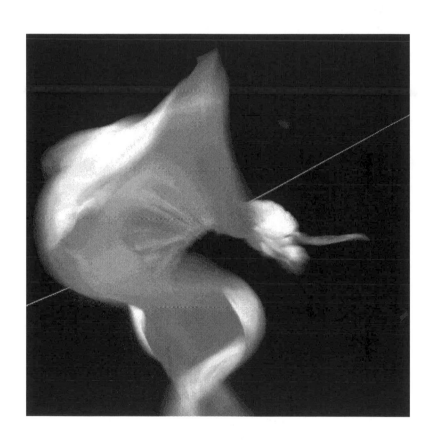

A Matter of Perspective

Hurry, hurry! I must make it.
Hold tight, walk just right.
Is this the door? Is that the door?
Men, Women, Ladies, Gents.
Girls in dresses and boys in shorts.
So many doors!
Here? No there! Not there! But here?
Did I try this door or that one over there?
Was I here or there?

At last! This is it! Doors!
Some are open. Some are closed.
Some with talking in them.
I squish my nose as I peek through the crack.
WHOOSH!
Oh what do I do?

I find an open door and push it closed.
It bounces back.
Push – open; push – open; PUSH – OPEN; PUSH - OPEN
Oh brother!

Around and around I step
Till I must step no more.
I grab the seat and plop – down, far down, oh so far down.
I hear tinkling.
Up come my pants, hands wet, shirt half tucked in, seams twisted
to the side.

Where are the handles?
Oh my! It's magic. Water sprays all over me.
Wave…spray…wave…spray…wave…spray
The lady glares at me.
Wave…spray…wave…spray…wave…spray
Oh brother!

I laugh at the lady waving like a butterfly at the wall.
Magic paper comes from the bottom.
She leaves and all is quiet.
I wave like a butterfly and magic paper happens again.
Then, I'm a butterfly flitting around the room.
Butterfly, butterfly, oh, where am I?

"Mom," a voice calls out.
"I'm here, come with me."
And the butterfly flew away.

"To care for those who once cared for us
is one of the highest honors."
Tia Walker, author

Things

Buttons and snaps and spools of thread.
Newspaper articles taped to the wall.
Doilies, tchotchkes and milk glass.
So much, too much, who wants such?

Would you like this?
Would you like that?
So many no thank you's
Caused her so many tears.
So much, too much, who wants such?

I took this and that and that and this.
After all, it's just stuff.
No more tears. Instead, peace in her eyes.
Her eyes once so wise.

Buttons and snaps and spools of thread.
Newspaper articles taped to the wall.
Doilies, tchotchkes and milk glass.

Treasures of this and that.
Of conversations and smiles.
Of every days and special times.
Of a house made a home.

So much, too much, who wants such?
I do, that's who.
Treasures passed
Of conversations and smiles.
Of every days and special times.

Backseat Drivers

They're backseat drivers.
You know the ones.
They sit in the backseat in their own world
While you chauffeur everyone around.
That is until you hit a pothole,
And everyone voices what you should have done.

Day in and day out you exhaust yourself.
Night after night you listen for her.
You tell yourself that tomorrow will be different.
That she just had a bad day.
That if you just paid more attention
You could make the day easier.
If you just had more patience she wouldn't get upset.
If you just remembered to make it all perfect,
She would be, too.

But that's your heart talking.
You know, the one that's broken.
Thoughts creep into your head that perhaps
She would be better – safer – somewhere else.
But what a betrayal that would be.
I'm a terrible daughter.
My sisters will tell you so.
It's not so bad.
You're exaggerating it all.
Mom doesn't seem that bad to us.

Are you nuts? Am I nuts?
What part of this don't they get?
Don't they see what's happening?
What right do they have to talk to me
About how I should have missed the pothole?
If they want to drive, well let them!
Let's just see how it works for them.

But you can't do that.
They don't get her like you do.
But if you get her then why are there thoughts of
Putting her on a bus that takes her to the unknown?

To where they don't know she hates tomatoes.
And that she sleeps in fuzzy pajamas,
And that she used to be a secretary,
And that she eats a cracker after she takes her medication,
And that she's afraid of the dark,
And that aqua and pink are her favorite colors.

Oh, it's tough. This isn't for sissies.
You'll stay awake worrying.
You'll call and tell them mom likes milk with her lunch.
You'll visit her and cry when you leave.
You'll see things aren't perfect.
You'll think your sisters are right and you put her on a bus,
A bus to a strange city where she knows no one.
You'll think you're weak.

Until one day you'll see her laugh.
She's drinking milk with her lunch.
Her fuzzy pajamas are in the laundry.
And they say she loves to dance.
Dance? I never saw her dance.
She's making a life.
Without you.

Oh, she'll probably beg to come home.
She might tell you you're an ungrateful, bad daughter.
It'll be hard to hear – from her and your sisters.
But when you can just visit her and be her daughter again
And not her nagging caretaker, your heart will melt.

You'll be strong and know your sisters can't see
The potholes from the backseat.
And you'll meet your mom,
And maybe you'll love her even more.

"I was so afraid to feel free to enjoy my own life if my mother was
sick and suffering everyday of hers.
I didn't think I had the right."
Gene Wilder

Lost and Found

Mom, where are your glasses?
Glasses? Do I wear glasses?
Are they in your pocket?
Let me look?
Let's search your room.
I'm sure we'll find them.

We look together.
Me for your glasses.
You, for whatever you find.
Lost glasses, that memory long gone.

You show me a shoe.
Nice shoe, but not glasses.
Again, I found them!
Mom, that's a hairbrush.
It is! Isn't that what you want?
What did you lose?

I didn't lose anything, mom.
You lost your glasses.
Glasses? Do I wear glasses?
Let me help you look.

Mom, here they are.
But where is my shoe?
We were looking for your glasses.
Glasses? Do I wear glasses?

Joe

Oh, that red headed little boy.
You know, he's a talker.
And his smile,
It's love straight from the heavens.

I think he'll be a lawyer.
Let's hope not a politician.
We talk about philosophical things.
Oh Joe.
Joe. Joe. Joe.

Oh, that red headed boy,
He's growing up so fast.
He's a talker.
And his smile,
It's love straight from the heavens.

I think he's one of John's boys?
He sits by my side and we talk.
"How was your day, Grandma?
Did you go for a walk?"
They say his name is Joe?
Joe? Joe? Joe?

Oh, that red headed boy.
I've seen him before.
He's a talker.
Come sit by my side.
They sit together in silence.
They say more without words than ever before.
And their smiles,
They're love straight from the heavens.

Mother's Day

It's Mother's Day, but for you it's any day.
I gave you a wrist corsage.
Pink and blue flowers – your favorite colors.
A card telling of my love for you,
And chocolates that would end up on your face for later.

You smiled when you saw me and I gave you smoochie kisses.
That was my Happy Mother's Day.
I didn't need anything else.
But, then like the turn of a dime, the joy was over for you.
You hung your head and began to cry.
I could see the pain on your face.
You didn't have anything for me.
You couldn't do anything for me.

I tried to tell you it was OK.
You would have no part in that and spit on me and slapped me.
Then you went away while sitting beside me.
I tried to bring you back but you were gone.
Lost in your thoughts or just lost with no thoughts except anger.

Your smile was my gift.
It was a generous gift to be cherished.
You had already given me everything.
I took a chance on making you happy.
It was iffy at best, but still I took the chance.

My feelings weren't hurt, but I was sad for you.
Sad that something else was gone from your life.
We won't celebrate any more holidays.
After all, what's a holiday but another day to share our love?
We don't need anything or any special day for that.
Every day is Mother's Day.

Shattered

Years of life filled days we'd retire.
Awaken again to times long ahead.
Dreams whispered.
Hopes shattered.
Newspaper puzzles undone.
Who will dust baby Jesus?
Blues mix with black without your eyes.
I walk forlorn while you cry for home.
A place no longer ours.
The same stars do you see as we lie alone?
No more love could there be as you fade away.
Shattered

Always

Will you remember me?
Will you love me?
Will you hold me tight?
When I forget, will you tell me?
Will you bathe me?
Will you feed me?
Will you pray for me?
Will you come see me?
Will you miss me?
Will you watch over my love?
Always?

Always

RRIIIIIINNNNNGGGG

Hello.
Are you there?
Yes, mom, I'm here.
Did you call me?
No, you called me.
Are you home?
Yes, you called me at home.
Why did I call?
I don't know.
You don't?
Let me help you remember.
Did I forget something?
I don't know.
Why did you call me?
You called me.
I did?
Yes, you did.
Hmmm, I don't know why?
Click

Like We Did Before You Forgot

We laugh together like we did before you forgot.
Of nothings that turned out to be everythings.
Of silver polish covered witch fingers
And make-believe screech talking.
All the while burning into my memories of smells
The heady aroma from the soft flannel cloths.

We laugh together like we did before you forgot.
Of dining room campouts with tablecloth tents.
Oreo cookies and milk around a flashlight so bright.
Giggles and wiggles and squirming like worms.

We laugh together like we did before you forgot.
Of your rescuing the sick little angel from the front of the church.
Just in the nick of time.
Oh, you knew what would happen,
But let me pretend I was fine.

We laugh together like we did before you forgot.
Tears in my eyes as I tell the stories.
No longer ours. Just mine.
The tales are cute and give you a laugh.
And tomorrow, I'll tell them again,
When we'll laugh together like we did before you forgot.

Two Last Voice Messages

Two of your voice messages
Saved as frozen moments in time,
When a dog was a tree
And day was night.

You called yourself dumb when the right words were gone.
I listen and silently scream that it doesn't matter
You say a car flies in the sky.

I replay your saved voice so beautiful to my ears.
I wish you knew that the words didn't matter.

Memories flood with tears as I long for messages long ago erased.
Regrets for not realizing what I had done.

I grasp for parts of you that let me think
Things are as they always were.
As they always will be.

Your voice no longer calls.
No more, "I just wanted to tell you I'm thinking of you."

Yet, there's so much love in hearing
A dog was a tree
And day was night.

Today was a Good Day

I saw the twinkle in your eyes.
We laughed and laughed at nothing at all.
Peanut butter and chocolate on your face.
Freshly mowed grass tickled your nose.
You held my arm as we walked the halls.
Hugs for caretakers all around.
Beautiful cards in the mail.
Hand massages with droopy eyes.
You blew me kisses through the door.
Today was a good day.

Me, Me, Me

Played under the cherry tree.
Dodged the dogs and rode my bike.
Saturday bologna and beans.
On the bus to work.   Married a man so handsome.
Type, type, type   Made a life of two.
                                        Moved away to worlds unknown.
                                        Goodbye to old, hello to new.
                                        Again, again, again

Children three, different,
Yet from me.
Teach and play.
Watch and learn.
Who will they be?   Sunday school teacher,
Of me, of me, of me   Classroom mom,
                                        Gerbils, ant farms, lizards,
                                        Plays and recitals.
                                        For three, for three, for three

Holidays, vacations,
Summers carefree.
Year after year
Till they were grown.   College,
Gone, gone, gone   Weddings,
                                        Grandchildren.
                                        From me to thee,
                                        My children three.
                                        Love for you, for you, for you

Is it morning?
Did you call?
Were you here, was I there?
Up or down, in or out.   Lost words, vanished thoughts.
Round, round, round   Hugs and kisses.
                                        Stay with me.
                                        With me, with me, with me

Was I There?

Sisters, brothers, mother, father.
I was there.
Children, grandchildren, nieces and nephews.
No life sweeter.
I was there.
My daughter is my sister.
My husband is my mother.
Here we go, here we go.
Was I there?

Ears from God

Did you ever think of the ears?
Most people don't until they do.
But ears have heard an entire lifetime.

They heard your mother's loving voice before you were born.
There were sister secrets and giggles.
The ABC's that helped you to read books exploring the world.
And music, sung in perfect harmony over dishes and laundry.

They heard declarations of love and a marriage proposal.
And wore beautiful pearls on your wedding day.
They heard the cries of your babies.
And the wondrous sounds of everyday life.
Horns honking, rain falling, birds singing.
A lifetime of sounds put together that tell your story.

They hear us whisper our love for you.
We know you can hear us even though you don't respond.
Handel's Messiah, beautiful hymns, stories of Jesus.
Your ears are still the connection to the living world.
To happiness and family and our love for you.

What was Coming

We chuckled at first when you repeated yourself.
You knew what was coming.

When you copied your beautiful letters so you'd remember
What you had written to your friends and family,
You knew what was coming.

When you called me ten times a day
In order to figure out what to do,
You knew what was coming.

When we took you to visit what would become your new home,
You knew what was coming.

When you stood there and we all cried
As we left you that first night,
It had come.

When you packed to go home day after day
Even though you didn't know where home was,
It had come.

When you stopped talking, walking and eating,
It had come.

When we lay you to rest,
It will be done.

Is it Afternoon?

What time is it?
It's 11:23.
Is it afternoon?
No, it's morning.
What time is it?
It's almost 11:30.
Is it afternoon?
No, it's morning.
Did you tell me the time?
It's 11:38.
Is it afternoon?
No, it's morning.
What time is it?
It's 11:46.
Is it afternoon?
No, it's still morning.
What time is it?
It's 12:01.
It's afternoon!
Yes, it's afternoon!

Waiting

I've had enough!
Enough of everything I can't control.
Medication, AGAIN!
Food I don't recognize or that I don't want.
People pushing me places in a wheelchair.
After all I can walk there by myself.
Time for bed, time to get up, time for this and time for that.
Where's my dad? He'll get it fixed. He'll tell them.

They treat me like I'm sick. I'm not sick.
They say I can't walk. Of course, I can walk.
They say I fell. Wouldn't I know if I had?
They say I have to stay, that I can't go home.
Did I do something wrong? Was I a bad girl?
I'll wait for dad. He'll know. He'll tell them.
He'll get it fixed.

I wait and wait and wait some more.
Steadily, I rock in the chair by the door.
Is that him? No. This time? No, again.
Time after time strangers walk by and smile.
Maybe he's not coming.
Maybe something happened.
Maybe he forgot. Maybe he's sick.

Finally, it's him!
His eyes shine bright when he sees me.
My dad is here. He came - to. see. me.
He says I look good. See, I'm not sick.
He takes me for a spin in my new ride.
He greets all of the strangers with smiles and hellos.
I'm a good girl.
Dad's here and he fixed everything.

Decisions

Today you sit with the others like it's any other day.
But today is anything like any other day.
You slept late and were cleaned up and dressed.
Morning medications given.
Maeza fed you cornflakes, your favorite.
Just like any other day.

But in a room down the hall,
Hard decisions were being made about your life.
Decisions that only God should make.
Yet there we were deciding your fate.
The fate of an 84 year-old life that still is yours.
All the while milk dripped down your chin.

Orders were written to stop all intervention,
Others for comfort care.
With the brush of a pen your future was sealed.
All as cereal was scraped off your chin.

The sun is shining. People are talking.
There are things to do and places to go.
Yet for us, today is anything like any other day.

I look into others' eyes and wonder what's wrong with them.
Don't they understand that today we decided your fate?
That every day you live is a day you defy the odds.
The significance of milk dripping down your chin.

Soon you'll rejoice in heaven.
You'll be free.
Our human decisions long since decided.
And no more milk will drip down your chin.

Last Watch

It's not long now.
Nothing you have to do.
But for me, there's so much left.

I have to memorize the curve of your eyebrows.
And the way the crook in your nose bends.
Your lips are pursed like they were when you had a thought.
There are little creases in your earlobes, just like mine.

I count four little freckles on your smooth, pale cheek.
Your hands are cold, purple and frail.
Blankets wrap you tight and I can see your toes
Pointing to the sides.
I know you. I could tell you all of this from memory.
But, I don't want to miss a single detail.
I must remember them all.

Brown eyes that are honey warm.
Beautiful white hair with just a bit of pepper in the back.
The collars of three shirts, soft and worn.
One plaid, one pink with flowers and the last soft white.
I know them.
I've sewn buttons on them.
I've smelled you in them.

I can't stop staring in this last watch.

Night of Hymns

It's night again and we're alone.
It's our special time.
Tonight I brought a CD of your favorite hymns
And The Christmas Story to read to you.

Be Still My Soul; the Lord is on thy side.
You look at me, your eyes are pleading.
Begging for touch, a connection.
You speak words I can't understand.
But your reaching out for love is undeniable.

Be Still My Soul; the hour is hastening on.
Your eyes close and a calm smile comes to you.
Peace, Peace Like a River plays next, just like it was cued.
Then All Things Bright and Beautiful,
Another hymn that could describe your life.

Your hands cover your eyes.
I can only imagine your thoughts.
Is there fear or sorrow or longing for what wasn't?
Are you at peace? Do you see Jesus?
Are you afraid of leaving dad with his grief?

The Lord is My Shepherd, the next hymn in line.
He is your shepherd. He will lead you Home.
This is My Father's World.
He is in control. Life is His plan.
He will take you in His arms.

Next the carillon peels a welcoming.
Come, come join me. Follow me.
Do not be afraid.

The voices blend together, then weave in and out.
Just as you weave in and out of our lives,
Letting us get used to your memory bit by bit.

I Trust I Will See My Savior.
Your hands are clasped as if in prayer now.
Breaths in and out. Here, still with the living,
But moving closer to the call of Jesus.

Swing Low, Sweet Chariot.
Comin' for to Carry Me Home.
The chariot is coming for you.
And oh what a ride that will be.
What joy you'll have to see the Lord.

Maybe there'll be a grand parade
With your parents, brother and sisters,
Friends and loved ones.
They wait for you, to welcome you.
Weep not for us.

Be Still, My Soul; when change and tears are past
All safe and blessed we shall meet at last.
And then,
It is Well With My Soul.

He's Ready

He says he's ready.
Ready for her stuff to be gone.
He can't keep looking at it all.
Remembering how she looked.

Her ruby red lips and snow white pearls.
The muumuu from Hawaii.
Firenze. Waving in black handmade leather gloves, soft like butter.
That straw hat and blue denim shirt,
You know the one in the beach photo.
All the kids making a muscle while eating pancakes.
What about her boots with the tall heels?
They took her to hear Bach and Mozart at the finest concert halls.
A lace collar – a gift from you, when her smile lit up your memory.

Winter coats to windbreakers.
Soft sweaters always folded inside out.
Skirts pinned to hangers and tissue paper between folds.
Padded hangers. No shoulders jutting out in spiky points for her.

He says he's ready.
Today he is.

Six Hundred Miles

Six hundred miles.
Those words mean so many things.
Vacations, old friends,
People returning to work. Going away to college.
But to me, those words loom ominous.
The last six hundred miles before her ashes are buried.
The last six hundred miles
Before all the pomp and circumstance is over.
Before there's nothing else to do for her but remember
And honor her life and memory.

Five hundred miles left. A bit of panic sets in.
She's been with you as you listen to her favorite music.
You're driving with her husband,
Your husband, and her dear friend.
Occasionally there are bursts of laughter
As someone tells a memory.
But it's the kind of laughter that mixes with tears.

Four hundred more miles.
You wish you could turn the car around.
Or, maybe you could be delayed due to an emergency.
You check for messages on your phone.
Praying that someone needs you more than she.
But there are no messages. No missed calls.
The miles and the memories fly by just like the cars.

Three hundred more miles. That's all. Just three hundred.
What do you do with that time?
You steady your breathing. You hold back the tears.
You wonder how long it'll be before you forget her voice.
What about the next generation and the ones after that?
How is it possible that they won't know her?
They won't even think of her.
She may as well be a roller skate key.
Who will be their role model?
That is the saddest thought of all.

Two hundred miles and suddenly he says the magic words.
She's already home.
She's with God and she'll be with her family in Michigan.
What could be more perfect?
What more could one want for her?
Now the tears are of joy, wonder and awe.
She's already home.
No other words could mean as much.

One hundred more miles.
Yep, just one hundred.
You can hardly wait.
The final ceremony. It'll be a celebration.
And those who never met her, well they'll get their chance.
For she's waiting for us.
Arms wide open. The smile and her love.
Fear not, she says. I will be with you through eternity.
Just like the Lord.

How's He Doing?

They ask me how he's doing.
"Appropriately," I say.
That's not what I really want to say, but it's my standard response.
They don't really want to hear what it's really like.
They don't want to have to think about how it really is.
"Appropriately," I say.

I really want to respond with asking how they think he's doing.
Or, if you really want to know, then visit him.
Talk to him.
Be his friend.
His love of nearly 62 years is gone from his life.
He intimately cared for her for six years.
His life is upside down.
He has to reinvent himself, without her.

He's exhausted. His mind needs a rest. His mind needs her.
There is final paperwork - wills, trusts, estates.
Social Security, voter registration, DMV.
Phone calls and thank you notes. On and on.
Her things, he wants them gone, just as she is gone.
She's not coming back.
SHE'S NOT COMING BACK!

Some don't know what to do when they see him.
Some avoid him like the pariah.
Some don't want to upset him.
Some don't want to face his reality.
Some don't want to see him facing his reality.
It's too awkward and painful.
Will he cry?
What should you do?

Be normal. Look him in the eyes.
Ask him if he saw the baseball game.
Has he read the latest in the newspaper?
Tell a joke.
It sure is hot outside – the weather,
Always a good conversation starter.
Tell him about what you're doing.
Ask him to dinner. Ask him to church.
Help him join back into life.
Let him know you miss her too.

Talk about her. It's not like she never existed.
Laugh with him when he tells stories.
Tell your stories.
Don't pretend nothing has changed.
Everything has changed.
Meet it head on.

It'll get easier they say.
Will he get used to her being gone?
Probably not.
But there are still things to do, places to go, people to see.
Some days will be filled with such sorrow his knees
Will hit the floor.
Some days she'll hardly be there at all.
It's what happens when you love someone with all your heart.
Would you want it any other way?

They ask me how he's doing.
"Appropriately," I say.

"Mourning is love with no place to go."
Anonymous

"He will wipe every tear from their eyes.
There will be no more death or mourning
or crying or pain,
for the old order of things has passed away."
Revelation 21:4

God Be With You Till We Meet Again

Written by Jeremiah E. Rankin (1880)
Composed by William G. Tomer (1880)

God be with you till we meet again;
by his counsels guide, uphold you,
with his sheep securely fold you;
God be with you till we meet again.

Till we meet, till we meet,
till we meet at Jesus' feet;
till we meet, till we meet,
God be with you till we meet again.

God be with you till we meet again;
'neath his wings securely hide you,
daily manna still provide you;
God be with you till we meet again.

Till we meet, till we meet,
till we meet at Jesus' feet;
till we meet, till we meet,
God be with you till we meet again.

God be with you till we meet again;
when life's perils thick confound you,
put his arms unfailing round you;
God be with you till we meet again.

Till we meet, till we meet,
till we meet at Jesus' feet;
till we meet, till we meet,
God be with you till we meet again.

God be with you till we meet again;
keep love's banner floating o'er you,
smite death's threatening wave before you;
God be with you till we meet again.

Till we meet, till we meet,
till we meet at Jesus' feet;
till we meet, till we meet,
God be with you till we meet again.

Made in the USA
Columbia, SC
07 July 2022